TEXT
FAILS
FROM
MUM

Send

TEXT FAILS FROM MUM

BLINK

bringing you closer

Published by Blink Publishing
3.25, The Plaza,
535 Kings Road,
Chelsea Harbour,
London, SW10 0SZ

www.blinkpublishing.co.uk

facebook.com/blinkpublishing
twitter.com/blinkpublishing

PB – 978-1-911274-41-4
Ebook – 978-1-911274-42-1

All rights reserved. No part of the publication may be
reproduced, stored in a retrieval system, transmitted or
circulated in any form or by any means, electronic,
mechanical, photocopying, recording or otherwise,
without prior permission in writing of the publisher.

A CIP catalogue of this book is available from the British Library.

Printed and bound by Clays Ltd, St Ives Plc

1 3 5 7 9 10 8 6 4 2

Text copyright © Blink Publishing, 2016

Papers used by Blink Publishing are natural, recyclable
products made from wood grown in sustainable forests.
The manufacturing processes conform to the
environmental regulations of the country of origin.

Every reasonable effort has been made to trace
copyright holders of material reproduced in this book,
but if any have been inadvertently overlooked the
publishers would be glad to hear from them.

Blink Publishing is an imprint of the Bonnier Publishing Group
www.bonnierpublishing.co.uk

CONTENTS

Send

MUM DOES NOT COMPUTE

Technologically challenged, clumbsy-thumbsy-mumsy, however you want to put it, the outcome is the same. You have signed up to a 24-hour contract even if you don't realise it. Hardened criminals have lesser sentences. If you have a mother — and, let's face it, which of us hasn't at one time or another? — it is understood you are there to provide comprehensive IT support. When you think about the things she's done for you over the years, maybe it's not such a bad deal after all. At least, until you get the request to show her how to turn on predictive text — for the third time.

Back   Contacts

How are you finding
the new phone
Your new smartphone.
HELLO!

howdoyoudoaspace

Send

Security At Its Best
Back
Contacts
I think my PC has been hacked!!
I'll have a look at it for you. What's your password?
password.
Yes, your password.
password.
That's what I keep asking.
I know. The password is password.
That would explain it.
Send

The Google

Back Contacts

Why have you changed the Google logo?

I have nothing to do with that. Google does that.

I liked the old one.

Can you ask them to change it back?

I don't have the emails for Sergey and Larry.

Who?

Never mind.

Send

That's Not What You Think

8===D

Love You!

That is not love

I don't know what you mean

8==D is a love smiley

It's a penis emoticon!

I think someone is having a laugh. Is this a love smiley hug?

8==D {()}

NO!

Send

Phone, What Phone?

Now I have lost my phone! Can you help?

Look at your hand.

I'm looking at my hand. I'm holding the shopping. Are you saying it's in the bag?

Think about it. What are you using to text me?

Never mind! I found it! Thanks!

Send

Laughing At Tim

Back Contacts

Tim is in hospital and it doesn't look good LOL.

Why are you laughing?

I'm not. What do you mean?

LOL means laugh out loud.

Oh no! I sent that to all my friends and Dad too. I need to call them.

Send

You Say It!

Back

Contacts

Got the promotion!

WTF!

Why do you say that? Don't you think I deserve it??

No, I was just saying
Well, Thats Fantastic
like you do all the time!!

Send

Bed Time From Hell

Back Contacts

I just got a missed call from you.

I'll call you back. I'm just fucking your brother in bed.

Oh, MUM! WTF?

Sorry, I meant tucking. That was the phone.

Send

Have you got a picture of that place you stayed in last year?

No, no, god!

Mum! Does Dad know you stayed there????

Send

Drunken Mum

When are you going out?

Inner fountain urn.

Were goingsee Stab Wars floating towers.

Haha. Mum! Are you pre-loading again? 😉

Fone u u.

Send

Back

Contacts

I have no idea where you are or what you're doing but those photos aren't working.

Never mind.

Send

How Can You Be Sure?

Back Contacts

You are better with tech than yur dad. How I check if my messages are getting thru??

Yes, it's fine

How can you be sure?

I'm reading one now

You reading it. So that means it's ok?

YES!

Send

Carpet Problems

Back Contacts

Cum in carpet

WTF?

Get cum out of carpet

THIS IS NOT GOOGLE

Sticky cum carpet

Sorry. Your brother trod
chewing cum into the carpet

Send

I worked out how to do hashtags

gr8

hashtag worked out hashtags

Send

What Does It Mean?

Will b back late staying at Syreeta's 4 food and lolz

What does lolz mean?

Laugh Out Loud

But what about the z?

Dunno doesnt mean anything?

Oh, ok

LOLZ!

Send

Back   Contacts

I am using Skype now

No, you're on the text

No

Is this Skype?

It's a text message

Why cant I see you?

Send

Doesn't Get Out Much

Back   Contacts

My friend Alfred is here. What was the name of that restaurant?

Er which one? Clue please.

The one we went to two weeks ago with the little food.

Little food? Do you mean the Mexican? With the street food?

Yeh.

Wahaca.

OK, I will put Alfred on. Can you tell him?

Send

Solitaire Instructions

Playing solitaire on the laptop

Sounds good

How do I make the cards move?

I think it might be too difficult to explain in a text

Send

Predictive Text Problems

Are we still going to family at wkend?

Yes, urinal uncle telephone tomorrow tornado

Sorry, we will leaven at lunar cycle

I problem

Can you turn off predictive text for a minute?

Send

eomfpe ;ovlrt

One first text for Mum!!!
1 giant text for Mum-kind.

What does it mean?

eomfpe ;ovlrt

Send

This Is Your Mother Speaking

Back Contacts

Is all going ok? From Mum.

Yes, fine and you don't need to tell me who you are.

Just wanted to be certain you knew who this is.

Look at the top of the screen.

It says your name!

Send

Children Always Know

What was that film they talked about on the news?

I don't watch much news.

Mum, you can use catch up on the TV to watch again.

Yes, I just thought you would know.

Send

Back   Contacts

hhow are you sweetie?

Are you 😄 or 😵
I have a pain in my 😄

Come over to eat with us
🍷 🍗 🍺 🧁

xxx!

Send

Ru cmng 2d? i need milk and bd can u?

Good to see U R getting the hang of txt but I literally have no idea what U R talking about.

Send

Hi, I just called you but you didn't pick up. I left you a message. Can u call when you listen to the voicemail and then we can talk on Skype?

Send

I put ur pudding in the cupboard in your room.

Could I have it in the kitchen?

That was the fone not me. I meant ur hoodie.

Send

Back

Contacts

Send space text to space my son full stop

You don't need to say space. Just say the words.

This the words is the words much the words easier the words than the words typing the words full stop

Send

Oops!

Vicky on fone totally hysterical about that stupid man.

I'll talk to her.

Why are you sending me this?

I don't kno what happened.

Mum, you've set up a group message.

I don't know what that is.

Send

Texting Troubles

How do I find someone's text address?

Same as the phone number.

Oh. How do they do that?

No, it IS phone number.

Even if I want to text?

Send

FB Friend Fail

Back Contacts

Would I want to get on Facebook?

No

What do you do on Facebook or Twitter?

Probably not that useful for you

Also you have problems with email, Mum

Could I be your friend?

Send

Siri Is Useless

Siri send text son oh

Call ma call ma

Siri son call old mum

Just use your thumbs LOL

Send

Blue Screen Of Death

Is someone trying to send me a funny message?

Pretty sure not.

What a relief!

www.howtogeek.com/163452/everything-you-need-to-know-about-the-blue-screen-of-death/

Send

This Is Your Child

Back Contacts

I feel really ill today. I'm going to take the day off work.

Wish you were looking after me!

Who is sending this?

Send

I see you are getting the hang of emojis.

There are too many. What are they all for?

Send

Explaining Abbreviations

Back

Contacts

What does TTYL mean?

I'll talk to you later.

No rush, just thought you might know.

Send

A Mother's Intuition

Someone changed the names in my phone.

Was it you?

How did you know, Mum?

As my son appears now to be King Kunta call it a lucky guess.

Is your dad Captain Twat?

I'm really sorry.

I think I can guarantee you will be.

Send

That's the kind of outfit I'm thinking of. U will look much smarter.

Did he know you took that photo?

Of course not! Secret! ;-)

You CANNOT take pictures of randoms.

It's OK if they don't know.

Send

HELP!

Back | Contacts

mUM

How's the new phone working out?

yest

I'll come over and help you with it tomorrow.

help

Send

Why Do We Do The Things We Do?

I Have Signed Up For A Monthly Contract Now.

Did you get a new phone too?

Yes. It Has A Big Screen And I Can Get The Internet And The Email.

Why are you putting capital letters at the beginning of each word?

I Don't Know.

Send

Back   Contacts

I can't type kill me now.

That makes no sense.

Every time I type kill me now it says kill me now. Kill me now.

I don't know what you're trying to say but I think your other child has been messing with the shortcuts. Love you!

That's what I was trying to say. Kill me now.

He's in a lot of trouble.

Send

A Mother Is Always Available

I can't talk at the moment.

I can't talk at the moment.

I can't talk at the moment.

I can't talk at the moment.

I can't talk at the moment.

I can't talk at the moment.

Hi Mum! Can you talk at the moment?

Of course I can. What do you want?

Send

Мы можем зделать

My Russian is rusty but I'm guessing you're saying you've selected a cyrillic alphabet and you can't turn it off?

Вам Каротажный

Are you planning to move to Moscow??

Необсаждённой

Laughing too hard! I will phone you on your landline to talk you through the settings, comrade!

Send

Back   Contacts

I just worked out how
to do shell fish

What are you talking about?

Ah

Send

Bring It Back!

I weld luuk u 2 tynn on aotoxorewt

cna u trun onn atuoxorevt

Are u asking me to help you turn the autocorrect on again?

ys

I thought you might regret changing that!!! :-)

Send

MUM JOKES

Send

There are times when your mum makes you crack up laughing without her having the faintest idea why, but sometimes she might even be having a joke at your expense. She may also be an expert in well-worn gags that her friends have told her and that she thinks you will never have heard. Mums have seen it all and heard it all – and more than anyone they know that whatever doesn't kill you will probably raise a smile.

Back Contacts

Mondays are like your father. They come too soon.

Oh, MUM!

Send

Cruel But Funny

Back　　　　　　　　　　Contacts

Mum! I can hear footsteps in the house.

Scared.

On way.

Go and hide in your cupboard. RUN!

I can hear them. Pls hurry.

Don't move.

I can't get out! I've been locked in!!!!

That was me home early haha.

Coming upstairs again now.

Are you still talking to me?

Send

Back

Contacts

I need to ask you something important.

What do you want?

Just wondered. What's up?

The ceiling.

You're really funny, Mum.

Send

MILF
Back
Contacts
Hey, you know your mum is actually very hot?
Really?
Yeah. I'd do her for sure.
I just picked up Ewan's phone. This is his mother. I find you strangely attractive. Why don't you come over now?
What? No, are you winding me up??????
Bring protection.
Send

Back

Contacts

Have booked 10 day hike in Peru!!!! YOLO!!

That's great, Mum, very exciting.

Didn't want FOMO!!

Are you just doing this to sound hip?

Bit old for all the slang.

FOAD!!!

Send

I'm still at Clare's.
Can you give me a lift?

Of course.

Thx xx

Your Uber mother is on her way.

Your Uber mother is getting nearer.

Ok, ok, I won't ask next time.

Your Uber mother is outside waiting where she won't embarrass you by being seen.

Send

Do you have sthg U need to talk to me about?

What's the matter?

Nothing. Just wanted to get you to respond to me for once. Xx

 XXxxXX

Send

Can you lend me some money 2nite 2 go out pls?

Delivery of this message failed.

Wtf? Is this u?

Delivery of this ungrateful child should also have failed.

U R very funny, Mum.

Send

You've Been Punked

Are you and David studying?

Yep.

He's not having a party?

No.

Not what it sounds like from where I am outside in the car.

Shit!

 Thought that would get you. See you later.

Send

Fridge Raider

Back Contacts

Did you raid the fridge again last night?

Yes, sorry, Mum.

Sorry about that.

I can't cook apologies.

Send

Age Is Just A Number

Happy birthday, Mum!

You still look great.

For your age.

LOL. luv u 2 Mum!

Send

DNA Test Wanted

Back Contacts

Can you give me a lift back from practice?

It's not far.

It's raining! Please!

I think askdf205;;*** some interference 09[asdfj****""' don't quite understand 002348**&dfdf:::: bad signal

I'll call you.

I can't believe you're my child. Is it too late to get a test?

Send

The warden is at the car now writing a ticket. This is a disaster.

Tell him you'll show him your tits.

LOL you are evil!

I'll end up paying it anyway.

Send

Your mum's like a library.

She's open to the public!!!!

Josh, this is Duncan's mother.

You don't think I ever look at my son's phone?

Very sorry, Mrs Fay. it wasn't about you, it was just like a joke. Sorry. Can I still come over later to see Dunc?

Of course. And don't forget…

Your mother is so ugly that when she's on stage at the strip club they pay her to keep her clothes on.

LOL you are the best friend's mum.

Send

Happy Valentine's Love Mum
Back
Contacts
Roses are red…
Violets are blue!!
You're the most wonderful…
…a face like yours belongs in the zoo.
MUM!
Send

Back   Contacts

I've made something just for you.

Guess what: begins with P and ends with ORN.

PORN?? What R U on about?

 It's safe to come downstairs now.

Send

Dead Man Walking

I was sooo embarrassed at the chemist but I've got them and I can't wait to see U 2nite.

I think this was meant for my daughter.

Make sure you put it on properly. We don't want her father to have to bury another boyfriend under the patio. He's running out of space

Sorry, Mrs Newell.

Send

I have done my test and I'm pregnant.

They're very advanced at that school then.

^^^perfect! I got a 100.

I'll stop knitting the booties, dear.

Send

I Am Not Above Bribery

We're leaving now. Look after yourself and the house.

I've left you £50.

Great, where is it?

Somewhere. Somewhere in YOUR ROOM.

Think about it this way. Tidy the room and you'll get £50!

Send

Calling Dr Who

Back	Contacts

Sorry I haven't been in touch. Phone died.

I was really worried about you. Anything could have happened! You must be more careful!

Sorry, I should have got a spare charger xx

I was about to set off the cloister bell.

Are you actually quoting Doctor Who now?

Things were bad xxx

Send

Mum Is Cooler Than You

Hi sweetheart. Are you going out over the weekend?

No, I don't think so.

Loser!

Send

I had a minor accident with the car but don't worry, I'm ok. And no hilarious comments please. You never make real jokes.

I made you.

Send

Back

Contacts

Someone came from the local leisure centre asking for a donation for the pool.

So I gave him a cup of water.

Good?

Haha, you is funny, Mummy.

Send

Adoption

Big news! Are you ready?

Yep.

Your sister was adopted.

What? Why are you texting me?

We're going to tell everyone. So just six months until she leaves!

I think you should look at your other text.

NO! She was accepted. By Cambridge!

You were the one who was adopted.

Joke

Send

Don't Push It

Are you ready with your ({}) for me?

Madhu's left her phone here but I can see this is Nish. What is ({}) please?

It means book. It's just what we say when we want a book.

I see. I'll tell you her when she gets back.

Thx can you also say I want to check out her (.)(.)

That means earrings.

I'm very X (and you might want to stay away tonight or you may be in danger of losing your 8==D.

Send

Pun-ny Texts

I'm hungary.

Do you feel like a frankfurter?

Or a hamburger?

LOL! I'm Russian to the kitchen.

Don't eat anything with too much Greece.

Send

Back   Contacts

Can I bring Kris back? We were going to bake some crack.

Of course. But I thought you cooked crack, not bake it? I forget the details, it's been so long since I did any really good drugs

Not crack, cake.

Really?

Send

Happy birthday, hope you're looking forward to coming home.

You've got presents waiting!!

Thanks, you're the best mum.

I know you wanted a rather special dress in blue by a certain Emilia Wickstead?

No! OMG that is totally amazing! You are THE BEST!!!

So, we bought you a bookmark in just that colour.

Send

Back   Contacts

> Come upstairs now. Massive daddy long legs dangling over the toilet door. Can't get out!

> HELP!!

> Really scary.

ELLO MY NAME IS BORIS.

I JUST ATE YOUR MOTHER!

WHAT'S FOR PUDDING?

Send

Bad news

What?

^ ^
> <
X

OMG my cat's dead!

No! That's her straining away as she pooed on your duvet.

Your mother is a talented artist. :-)

Send

Will you be visiting us
at the end of term?

Of course! If it wasn't so far,
I could come down earlier.

If you weren't such a mudblood, you
could transfer to Hogwarts and then
you could take the broomstick.

I haven't read Harry Potter
in a long time.

Doubt I'll ever forget it.

Send

Have you tried chicken tarka? It's like chicken tikka but a little otter. Laugh out loud!

You don't need to say laugh out loud. Type LOL.

Oh.

And that was a terrible old joke.

But did you laugh out loud?

Send

HOME LIFE

Send

We spend a lot of our time with our mothers – well, they're like one of the family. That's why fails with Mum are often a result of those mundane domestic incidents that make up daily life. It's where you can gather the most common examples of mix-ups and miss-keys that turn a catastrophe into a comedy. She may be telling you off, getting the better of you or just checking up that the house hasn't fallen down yet. Sometimes she's just telling you about a moment in her day that, frankly, makes no sense to anyone – probably not even her. Yet no one else can pull it off with such effortless style, if not grace.

Dr. Seuss

Back Contacts

Did you oops in the sink?

I mean did you poo on the shrink?

What?

On the shower.

Phone isn't working properly.

Did you poo in the shrink?

s h o w e r.

I didn't poo in anything. Shower, sink or shrink! Have you turned into Dr. Seuss?

Send

Did you get caught in
the rain today?

I hope you got to school OK?

Will you wash your hair tonight
before we go to see everyone?

We're going to take you to
Euro Disney this weekend.

OMG! Luv u!

No, we're not. Just wanted to make
sure you were getting my texts.

Send

Rude

Back Contacts

I'm pregnant. It must be something in the air.

Yeah, your fucking legs!

Send

Back

Contacts

I'm not coming back in after that. Fuck off!

It's about time. Your father and I thought you'd never leave. You need to get your own place.

No, Mum, that wasn't meant for you. What's going on? Well, fuck you too!!!!

I'm doing spag bol tonight. Love you. Don't be late.

Send

Smart Arse
Back
Contacts
Can I borrow £100 for the school trip?
NO! Do you think our money grows on trees?
What is money made of?
Paper.
What is paper made from?
Don't be clever.
Send

Answer Me!

Back Contacts

Mum, can you pick me up tonight?

What time can you pick me up?

I just met a girl and got her pregnant.

I'm throwing you out.

I knew that would make you answer me.

Send

Did you just phone me?

Yes, I wanted to talk to you in person. You're old enough to talk sensibly about sex, I think. That's what I wanted to say.

Sure. What do you want to know?

Send

What Have You Done?

Back Contacts

I don't say I luv u enuf.

What have you done?

I backed into the wall in the car park at Tesco.

You're grounded. You can't use the car ever again.

Send

Fish And Chip Fiend

Back Contacts

Can we have fish and chips for tea 2nite?

Is your fone on? Mum, I want fish and chips. Can you get some when you come home?

You never give me anything.

That's no way to ask for a treat.

I think I hear a burglar, Mum.

Ru being serious?

Yes, he says he's going to steal the telly unless you bring us all fish and chips.

Send

Forgetful

Back Contacts

Did you forget something this evening?

What do you mean, sweetie?

Who's in the back seat?

Oh no, I'm so sorry. Tell the school I'll be there in 10.

Yeah. Thanks.

Send

Back

Contacts

Rly sorry but I got suspended today.

OK, it was becos I threw a chair at Mr Pipprell in sociology.

Mum? I'm sorry. Pls answer.

It's been hours, say something.

My battery was dead. But thanks for being honest.

You're grounded for a month.

Send

Why Ask?
Back
Contacts
Do u think I'm old enuf to have sex now?
Sure. Why not?
No, I wasn't being serious.
Too right
Send

Can I buy a bikini now?

Yes, you haven't got much to cover anyway.

Send

The Hard Truth

There is no food left at all. Why haven't we got anything to eat?

Look down.

Yeh?

Can you see your feet?

No.

That's why, lard arse!

You're just jealous because my moobs are bigger than your boobs.

Send

I don't feel well.

Sorry.

No.

Do you want to call hospitality?

Can you bring me some Lemsip?

Send

You Want What?!

Do you need anything for the party?

Nice of u to ask. Can you get anus wrapping paper?

I'm not sure I will be near that kind of shop!

What?

I see what u mean, sorry.

Phone.

Meant ANY.

Send

Wishful Thinking
Back
Contacts
Text men later and let me know who you are doing!
LOL I wish!
Send

Can you call me?

Call pls.

Not right now. R U OK?

What is the name of that actress from Game of Thrones I like?

Send

Amanda Who?

Amanda has just got a new job! She's a director now.

No idea who you're talking about.

You know! Amanda.

Doesn't sound familiar x

Daughter of a friend of my friend, Kate.

Congrats to your friend's friend's daughter!

I just thought you might be interested.

Sorry, Mum. Love u.

Send

Hi Mum. I'm in the car park at Lidl.

Mum!

MUM, WHERE R U?

Home. Thought u could use some exercise.

LOL.

Send

Why Can't You Be Like Susan?

Did you have tea with your new neighbour?

She has a wonderful daughter, Susan.

Susan is always visiting. She's a solicitor and she does so much for everyone in our community. She makes the manager work much harder.

I admire her so much.

Shame your own daughter is so useless.

I wasn't saying that!!

U R so paranoid.

I know you are very busy with your own life.

Send

Urgent. Just ducked in toilet. Need to ask U sthg.

What is it?

One of my friends was talking about Dad. What's a metrosexual?

Send

Not The Favourite Child

Back   Contacts

Don't forget my birthday.

Again ;-)

What do you want?

What would you get me if you had unlimited money?

A phone without my number in.

Send

Predictable

Back Contacts

Are you on your way?

Still on way, just like
last time u texted.

Sorry, such a burden.
U will miss me when I'm
pushing up the daisies.

That's also what u always say.

Love u, Mum xx

Send

Back   Contacts

Don't forget Mother's Day.

Every day is Mother's Day.

NO. This Sunday.

Sunday is Mother's Day.

Right. Understood!

Send

Back   Contacts

Emergency. Come to kitchen asap.

R U OK?

Do washing up or call yourself an ambulance!

Send

Anything you want to eat?

I'll tell you what I want, what I really, really want.

So tell me what you want, what you really, really want.

Haha! Can I have a burger please? You're the greatest!

I know ;-)

Send

A Parent's Priorities

Hi Mum. How are you doing?

It would be really nice to see you. I'll pop over tomorrow night and we can spend some time together.

No. Watching the Strictly final.

Oh right. Sorry to crash your busy schedule.

Send

Happy anniversary to you both.

Thank you, darling.

Call me about a pic of you on Facebook.

Send

Clean Up After Yourself

How is the babysitting going?

Fine. I'm just bullying Abby.

Lovely. Make sure you mop up the blood!

Send

You Know Who I Mean

Hi. Don't you think that Jesse Eisenberg was over the top? He was far too young to be Lex anyway. He was trying too hard to be that other actor. What's his name? Died.

Heath Ledger.

That's the one. Thanks.

Send

Like Father, Like Son

I have just found your porn folder on the computer. We need to talk.

Sorry, sorry, sorry. Am I grounded?

That was meant for your dad but we need to talk too.

And yes.

Send

The Cheek!

Please make sure you tidy up your room tonight in good time before they get here for dinner.

I did not realise that we were hosting dinner in my bedroom. Shall I set a silver service?

And don't be a cheeky bitch!

Send

Un-Friend

Back Contacts

Who is this? My mate took my phone and said he was going to change all the names to their job descriptions.

What am I then?

Sorry, but it says prostitute.

This is your mother!

Which friend is responsible for this???

Send

I'm In Need

Back Contacts

Where is the vibrator! I'm in desperate need Paul!

Uhhhh… MUM!!!??? This is your Daughter! AND I DON'T WANT TO HEAR ABOUT THIS STUFF. FFS

Oh shit, sorry Sarah! Your Father and I have code names. Vibrator means soap.

Sure it does. You're disgusting, I will be back tomorrow.

Paul, I accidentally just texted Sarah, I thought it was you! Do you know where the vibrator is?

REALLY MUM? I'M MOVING OUT!

Send

It's My Job To Tell You

Will you be back in time to join us all, sweetie?

I'm really just too fat.

Nobody will notice and you did say you'd joined the gym.

Meant too FAR.

What do you mean? So I am too fat???

Oh.

Anyway, only your best friend and your mother will tell you these things.

Send

TOO
MUCH
INFORMATION

Send

There are some things we don't want to know about our mums. Let's be quite clear and specific here – it's mainly the stuff they do with our dads when we aren't around. What goes on behind bedroom doors should ideally stay there. The same rule applies in reverse. You may think your mum wants to know everything about you but she really doesn't. So how exactly does this classified data escape? Extensive research has revealed that oversharing, mistyping and alcohol mainly cover it. No matter how much bleach you scrub into your eyes, there are some texts you may never be able to unsee. But don't really rub bleach into your eyes, obviously. Sorry, that's beginning to sound like your mother!

Abstinence Is The Key

Back Contacts

I'd like to wake up with your face between my legs every morning ;-)

Oh god!

Mum, don't read that.

Too late.

Who is this latest squeeze?

I can't get into this now.

Yes, well, wish you said that last night.

Send

Spelling Is Important

Don't come home for a while.
Your dad and I areabouto fuck.

Did you mean to send me that text?

SORRY! *ARE ABOUT TO* FUCK

Send

Yeh... That's What You Meant

Hi Moira! Last night was great fun! You scream louder than anyone! Let's bang again soon, K?

Mum, not Moira! Don't want to know about your sex life. Or even that you have one at your age.

No worries, Mum. We were at the fair with our mates and me and Moira went on the drop tower and I just meant hang out, not bang. Not yet anyway ;-)

Send

MY EYES!

Back   Contacts

Can you come home early today?
I really need a good seeing to and
I've been soo bad.

I don't even want to
admit I read this.

NO, THAT WAS FOR DAD.

I did guess. Does that
mean I can stay out late?

No!

Send

129

Like Mother, Like Daughter

I thought you should know that I'm pregnant.

That's nice, darling. So am I.

Send

Back   Contacts

We have arrived at the beach.
Your dad seems very keen.

You have to stop sending me
pictures like this, Mum, I'm serious.

          Send

The Price You Pay For Children

Looking fwd to seeing you next wknd, love you

I love you too, Mum, U R the best.

Always love u, for ever and from the moment u and ur brother were born.

Even tho my pelvic floor never really recovered.

Ugh!

Send

Mum Thinks Of Everything

Don't do too much today.
Stay home and rest.

I left orange juice and
chicken soup in the fridge.

And I put tissues by the
bed in case you need
to blow your load.

Love Mum.

Send

Kinky

Back Contacts

Hired graduation gown and mortar board. What do I wear with it?

I went nude.

Eew, Mum!

Crotchless panties and a suspender belt.

I asked Dad, he says he wore same.

Send

Too Much Info

I just had a smear test.

Have you ever had a mammogram?

Your dad gives me one three times a week.

Send

Back

Contacts

Can you give me some ideas for what Daddy wants for bday?

That's revolting!

Anyway, I meant what he wants, not you ><

Send

Down With The Lingo

Back   Contacts

Hi Mum. Did u have a good weekend?

Your dad and I just netflixed and chilled.

Right. U kno that means having sex?

Yes ;-)

Send

Back   Contacts

I have finished banging with sarah, b home soon.

That's a coincidence – I finished banging with your dad too. What were the chances?

LOL! I meant hanging!

R U serious?

I won't tell if U won't.

Send

I am going to get you after school.

Who did u mean to send that to?

This is not appropriate behaviour.

She called me a slag and said that I took after u and that everyone knows you were a prostitute. She said her dad said that. It's not true, is it?

WTF! What an utter bitch. Kill her! Kill her!

Send

K

I have just offered you a whole evening out, including food and cinema, and you can only manage one letter? Is that what I carried you around for 9 mths for, pushed you out of my body and looked after you even though you wrecked my tummy muscles for ever?

OMG!

That's two more, I suppose.

Send

Blue Balls
Back
Contacts
I just found a pic of you holding your blueballs!
You were so adorable!
I don't recall ever taking that picture mom!!!
Please reread that msg!
I wrote boombox! What is a blueball?
Ask Dad
Send

We find it hard enough to keep track of what we've got to do by the end of next week. How are we supposed to give a full schedule for settling down and producing a suitably impressive number of grandchildren? Such undeniable and reasonable points will not deter many mums from stepping on to the love-nudge spectrum that runs from subtle hints to full-on dating service.

You could be in an important meeting or just about to take a key exam but if Mr or Ms Right is on the radar – or even just ambling unaware on the other side of the street – expect a text. Just don't always expect it to make sense.

I'm out with some of my friends from book group and Janine has brought her daughter.

Good for Janine's daughter!

She is a LAWYER.

So?

Will u leave me alone!

Just trying to help u, Darling. It's not nice to be alone.

Send

Easy Mistake To Make

Back Contacts

Hope you're not too sad. You'll find someone. I remember the day I first took your dad in my ass.

Ew! LOL

What?

Oh! No, I meant in my ARMS. Arms not ass.

Don't trust this phone.

I know!

Send

Back   Contacts

Sorry you're sad about breaking up. My Mum always said if a woman takes your man, fuck her best friend.

Are you sure Grandma said that?

Send

Bladder Issues

I have bought you a couple of thugs for Valentine's Day.

You really want to keep those boys away from your little daughter, yes?

I meant to say I bought you things!

I'm crossing my legs now, I am laughing so much.

Don't wet yourself, Mum! Haha!

Send

How did the party go?
You had some nice
pictures up on Facebook

Who was the nice young
lady next to you in the foto?

I don't think I've met her yet?

Send

Lovely here, very hot. We saw some flamenco dancing in the street.

Wow

The men are very dishy.

I said hello to them. Told one my daughter is 30 and still single. 😉 😉 😐 😉

Right.

U should come out here. 👍 👍 👍

Send

Don't Joke!

Are you still on the date?

Is it going well?

R U OK?

Yes, all fine, call l8r.

Is this you?

What was the name of your grandma's dog?

Stop txting me.

Molly.

I haven't been murdered.

Yet.

You won't be joking when you are murdered.

Send

Safe Sex

Back

Contacts

We will be away this wknd.

That's ok. I'm going to stay over with Nicole on Sat.

Thanks for telling me.

What is it your dad says?

Before you bag her, sheath your dagger.

MUM!

Send

Did you go home with that man you met last night?

If you're asking if I slept with him, I do have some standards actually.

Really. When did U decide to get those?

Thanks. :-/

Send

It Can Happen

How was the film?

We didn't go. He said he had some lovely puppies to show me. Dunno why he had to tie me up in this cellar to show them!

U shouldn't even joke about that. IT CAN HAPPEN, U KNO.

Mum, we are still watching trailers.

Send

Will u meet?

Come on, wot is the worst that can happen?

No conversation, different opinions on everything or I have to climb through the pub toilet window to escape him.

Knowing your luck, probably all of the above ;-)

Send

Hi Michelle

Who is this?

That was your mum. I'm Jake, I play rugby for Durham Uni and I was out with the team for a dinner. We just met your folks and your mum made me text you from my phone. She thinks we should meet up.

You have a great mum.

She totally kicks ass.

Send

Back

Contacts

Roses are red

Violets are blue

It's Valentine's Day

And ?? Loves you

Thanks, Mum. I feel better.

How did you know it was me?

Send

You will know if you love her period.

Interesting image, thanks!

I need to work on my commas but you need to work on getting me a grandchild.

Send

Wrong Child

Back Contacts

I couldn't wait to tell you!!!
I am pregnant! 😍

Why couldn't you at
least tell me in person?

Who is the father?

Simon, of course. My
husband!!!! Who did you think?

Sorry, I thought you
were your sister. Sorry.

Can we start this again?

Send

Shall we go out for a romantic dinner on Valentine's?

XXx your hypothetical girlfriend.

Thanks for making me feel good :-(

Send

Too Late

Back Contacts

You can't go on Facebook and like Paula's picture!!!

I've only been out with her twice!

I didn't know I had! Can I delete the like? Can you show me?

Forget it.

Send

We can meet at Pizza Express at 7. R U going to bring Ariadne?

Her name is Andrea.

You know I'm not good at using this phone.

And anyway, it's hard to keep track of all your girlfriends.

I knew you were thinking that!!!

Send

You Need Professional Help

Back Contacts

How did last night go?

Romance?

Did you finally get to kill him?

Kiss, sorry, darling xx.

You stop texting now or maybe you need to book in with that therapist at last.

Send

I Don't See A Ring

We are eating a bit early 2nite.

OK.

Are you bringing the deflowerer?

My boyfriend's name is Luciano.

While he's still just a boyfriend, he's the deflowerer.

Send

I'll Take What I Can Get

Ready for some good news?

Tamsin got the job! Lots of travel and she's managing a team.

So you're not going to have another child?

Not right now. Can U be happy being a grandma of one?

I'll take whatever my son gives me.

Send

OXFORD!

Back   Contacts

Kate I sat next to the nicest young man at Starbucks today. Oxford. Lawyer. I showed him your Facebook picture and gave him your number.

Mum you can't give my number out to strangers.

OXFORD!

Send

MUM DOESN'T LIKE TO WORRY, BUT....

Send

It is always reassuring when we know that Mum has our back. Unfortunately, sometimes she has our front and sides too. They don't mean to be overbearing or unduly cautious but then they wake up at 5 am in a panic because they've just remembered that the forecast for today was snowy, which means ice, which means slippery pavements, which means you'll be slithering around in those unsuitable shoes, which means… an emergency text. And you know how those always turn out. Well-meaning without necessarily meaning anything, the advice we get from our mums is, to put it kindly, unique.

Overly Cautious

Have you seen the news?

They think there is a bomb in the centre of London.

Maybe you should not travel today.

I should be ok here. In Manchester.

Send

Just seen the weather report. Make sure you wrap up. Wear that big sweater and be careful on the streets. I hope u r not cycling, u kno how dangerous it is. I don't like to think of u slitherIng around on that bike. There are 2 many lorries and if it rains, u will be in trouble.

Have a good day.

Send

Are you still feeling poorly? You shd call in sick. Give jo ur number, she can chk up on u.

I just have a cold. Jo has my number, we share the flat. If I die on the carpet she'll be the first to notice.

Send

ONE TONE

Back Contacts

HAVE YOU BOOKED
UR TICKET HOME?

You don't need to shout. I will.

I AM NOT SHOUTING??

I NEED TO KNOW WHEN
U ARE COMING BACK.

Send

Back   Contacts

Are you OK?

Call me!

Why?

What's wrong?

I just had a nap this afternoon and I had a dream that you were in Wales and you climbed a mountain and fell off.

I am in my house, watching TV. Love you, Mum xx

Send

Eager Beaver

Back Contacts

What time are you going to be here on Xmas eve?

Do you like sprouts?

Are we giving her presents?

It's 6 am.

I've been up for hours!

I'm making choc truffles with some burnt choc cake.

It's also a Sunday.

And it's the 18th of November.

I know! Not long now :-D

Send

Back   Contacts

> I finished my 10k in under an hour!

> You know I don't like you running.

> It's good for me and ud moan if I didn't do any exercise.

> I wouldn't like to be your knees.

> I wouldn't like you to be my knees either.

Send

Did You Know?

Back   Contacts

Have you seen the report about India? Risky for women.

http://www.dailymail.co.uk/travel/travel_news/article-2960567/Most-dangerous-holiday-destinations-women.html

Have a good trip love Mum xx

Wow, thanks a lot!

I just want you to be safe.

Remember, it's not Margate.

Send

Back   Contacts

How was the party?

Great, but I'm suffering today.

WTF is that?

That's my ecstasy dance of death! :-)

It's just because I'm your mother and I worry.

Mum, I don't do drugs.

Send

Appreciate A Good Laugh

Back   Contacts

Why have I got a missed call from the school? I can't get through to them now.

I got into trouble.

Now I am very nervous.

I was in geography and the teacher was telling us that the population density of Canada is 9 per sq mile and I said they must be lonely. Detention.

LOL! That is quite funny. That Mr Tinch has no sense of humour.

Send

Don't forget we're going to see your aunt after school.

Don't walk home.

I'll meet you at the gate but be on time.

Mrs Daniels, this is Gus's teacher, Mr Robertson. Please be aware that it is a school rule that mobile phones should not be used while students are in the classroom. I am confiscating your son's phone for a fortnight.

Now I know why Gus hates you.

Send

You Need A Holiday

Back Contacts

Look after the house properly. This is a big responsibility.

I know, don't worry! xx

When you go out, always doublecheck the cock.

You definitely need a holiday.

LOL

Send

Boy Who Cried Wolf

How is the decorating going? R U taking it easy?

I fell off a 20-foot ladder today.

Why didn't you tell me earlier?

Are you OK?

No worries.

I was only on the first step.

When you really hurt yourself don't expect sympathy from me.

Send

Look forward to seeing you l8r.

Going to be heavy traffic on the motorway so don't go too fast.

YOLO

That's not generally supposed to be such a bad thing.

Send

Back   Contacts

Make sure you are back by 9 2nite, OK?

Hello? Can you let me know you are OK. Back by 9.

It is now 9:30. Where R U?

You can come back at 11:30.

Thanks! Love u, Mum xx

Now I know u r reading this, get home now! You are grounded, btw.

Send

I'm not saying we haven't heard from you much but

Are you

1 Alive?

2 Dead?

3 Alive but unable to communicate?

4 Alive but have taken on secret mission for MI6 and unable to confirm or deny 1 or 2?

5 None of the above.

Send

Back   Contacts

Hope you are doing well.

I'm OK, are you at the hospital?

What?

That's a doctor wearing a mask.

Thought it was a big grin. I'm fine!

Send

Dad and I have been busy choosing colours for the bathroom. He is determined to do everything himself so it will take months if not years 😔

Also, Grandma would like a call from you if that's OK. Don't just email her but you could Skype. She would like that even more, you know what she's like.

I've got two big cases on at the moment, I'm going to have to do a tribunal in a month and then we've got the holiday coming up and I hope we shall be seeing you???????? How is everything at college?

OK.

Send

Typical

Back | Contacts

Monday 21:03

Are you OK? Where are you?

I'm out.

Who with?

A friend.

What time are you coming back? It's getting late.

Yeh, u should go to bed.

Do you need a lift?

Give it a rest!

Monday 23:57

Can you pick me up now, please?

For goodness sake!

Coming. Where are you?

Send

We arrive on the campus before lunch. What time is the ceremony?

Great. It's 3:30

Have you seen this news report? 50,000 new graduates are in jobs that don't need degrees, like hospital porters and lollipop ladies. Very worrying.

www.independent.co.uk/student/career-planning/thousands-of-graduates-working-in-jobs-that-dont-require-any-qualifications-a7114056.html

Thanks

Send

COMMUNICATION BREAKDOWN

It's not all one way with text fails. Even the best-worded updates can go awry to, as well as from, Mum. A misspelled word here and a rushed message there and suddenly we fall into a very strange and different world quite by accident. Language we would never dream of using in front of our mother or hearing from her is suddenly right in front of us and impossible to delete. We spend all that time encouraging our mums to join the 21st century and then we find ourselves regretting it when they do.

Anniversary Gift

Back

Contacts

I am divorcing your dad!

What now?

He gave me a stiffy for our anniversary.

Too much information!!!!

Not a stiffy! A Swiffer. 20 years of marriage for a Swiffer.

What is a stiffy?

Don't even ask. But it's better than a Swiffer.

Send

Affair With The Neighbour

Going out with next door.
Dinner is in the microwave.

Excellent. Thanks!
Where are you going?

He's going to show me his cock.

WTF! Why are you telling me that?

No, no. HIS COCK.

Yeah, got it, thanks.

D O C K, where he keeps his boat.

Send

Nevermind

Back Contacts

I did you a packed lunch today for your brother. It's in the fridge.

I knocked his dick over so watch out it doesn't spurt everywhere.

What now?

I mean his d r I n k. It is fizzy and. Nevermind.

LOL. Thanks.

Send

Can you pick up a takeout menu from the pizza place on the way back?

OK!

Food has gone wrong. Had a Taliban explosion in the kitchen.

^^^ Italian.

Could be Taliban too.

Send

Are you still coming over for dinner? What do you want?

I'd like a sausage in my pussy.

No! I mean I'd like sausage. In my pussy.

P A S T A.

One special coming up, LOL!

Send

Are you still bringing your friend home?

Yes. And my friend is drunken

Well, don't bring him back here! I don't want your drunk mates here, Emma.

I mean DUNCAN. I was just telling you his name!

Send

Time For A Quickie?

Back Contacts

Mike says he's coming home today. Do you want to skive off for a quickie?

Mum. This is Mike. You're texting your SON FFS.

Oh sorry, I was just saying that we should quickly clean up the house.

I can come home tomorrow.

NO! Today is fine.

Looks like Mike is coming back later so you need to be fast.

MUM, IT'S STILL ME. RIGHT I'LL COME BACK TOMORROW THEN.

Send

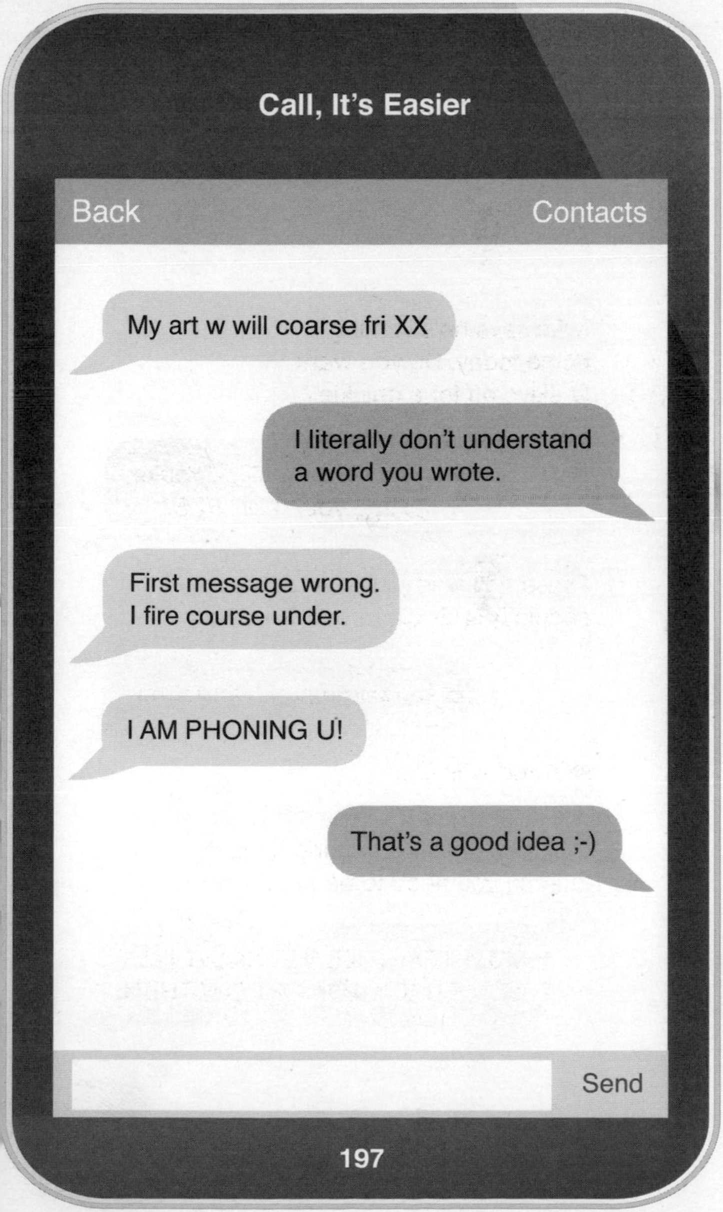
Call, It's Easier
Back
Contacts
My art w will coarse fri XX
I literally don't understand a word you wrote.
First message wrong. I fire course under.
I AM PHONING U!
That's a good idea ;-)
Send

Will be staying in office to do some male, tell your Father.

4 real?

Stop messing around, just do what I say.

Dad says you have to leave home, he is very upset.

MAIL, not male. I meant post. Letters.

I'll phone Dad myself.

Send

Cheese, Please?

Are you back from France yet?

Yes. We flew in this morning.

Did you manage to get any more of that dick pus cheese?

Not dick, delicious.

Sorry!

LOL! Yes, we got the cheese and not the pus. You can have some when we come over at wkend.

Send

The Severity Of Sausages

Good news!

You are buying me a new bike?

No, your grandma has the all-clear.

gr8!

The tests show it was just her sausages is inflamed.

Oesophagus.

Haha, she wouldn't want irritable sausages!

Send

Typo Trouble

Back Contacts

Just so you know, I've got a class coming to beast feed.

What?

In the mouse. Be later today so don't be embarrassed.

Confused, Mum!

Breast feed in the house, LOL!

Send

Why, Mother, Why?!

R U feeling better?

Not really.

Just talking to next door –
she says a dildos going round.

BAD COLD

😮 why is that on
your autocorrect?

Send

The Best Stocking Filler

If you come for Xmas, you can have your stocking.

You might find you get chocolate penis.

Not penis, penis.

P E N N I E S

I might prefer a chocolate penis.

Don't be vulgar!

Send

Look who we are sitting next to!

A napkin?

Coleen Nolan!!!!!

I think she heard the photo click noise.

She looks cross.

Send

We Love You, No Matter What

I just wanted to tell you that I'm coming out.

I always knew, so did your dad. We still love you.

I pressed send by mistake. Not gay. I meant I'm coming out to see you when you're in Spain this year.

Ha! We still love you.

Send

Dad's already in bed so when you come in tonight, be quiet and don't forget to lick the door behind you.

Won't that make it all wet?

Fine, I'll lock the door myself and you can go and live somewhere else.

Send

Back Contacts

I'm OK for now, I finally got laid.

You wot?

I got P A I D… no need for loan.

Good. I was going to say I did too!

You've been paid?

Yep.

Send

Grandma's Randy

I have no idea what to get Grandma for Xmas.

She would appreciate anything that shows some thought. What about a nice horny man?

That won't do anything for her blood pressure.

I meant ornament, but she probably wouldn't say no!!!

That's a terrible thought to have about your own mother!!!!!

Send

The Need For Speed

Have you done the speed yet?

I didn't know you had even heard of amphetamines.

Done the DEED!!!

Don't stress out, I've sent off the application.

Now I'm going to do some speed.

Send

Birthday Surprise

Back Contacts

Your brother says he wants us to buy him a banana hammock for his birthday.

Weird as usual. He doesn't even eat fruit.

Haha!!!

What?

Google it.

Oh!

Send

Back   Contacts

Will you text me when you get in? No willies in the house.

Harsh!

Wellies. It's wet out there.

LOL…

Send

Next door at Farah's and I must say she has no control over her pussy! It dribbled everywhere. Awful stench and it made me all sticky.

Puppy! Farah has new puppy.

I think I might have peed myself. :-)

Please don't tell her or her daughter.

Send

Put Off Your Food

> I'll be back after swimming for lunch. What are you doing?

I've got some delicious-smelling pantles.

Or would you prefer pasties? ;-)

> I am totally not hungry any more. U are banned from texting.

Send

Chicken À La WHAT?

Back Contacts

Thanks for cooking us both dinner. What was in the chicken? It was really tasty!

Quite a bit of harissa, red wine vinegar, salt and ground black people.

I didn't have you down as a cannibal racist.

Pepper! I am so sorry, darling.

Send

Not Legal

It was a bit sad. I watched your sister fondle herself last night.

Nothing came up.

That doesn't sound legal to me.

No! She Googled herself.

She's not that popular.

I'm not now.

You are with me! LOL

Send

Back　　　　　　　　　　　　　　　　Contacts

Can't make it to yours tomorrow, darling.

I'm going to have to devour a baby.

This doctoring is hungry work.

I hope you are better at the medicine than the typing xx

Send

Terrorist Alert

Making a change to my will.

Are you feeling OK?

I want you to know that I'm leaving some money to isis.

They are close to my heart.

What are you talking about?

Crisis! The homeless charity. Now I am worried about the phone reporting me a terrorist.

I'll come and visit you in Guantanamo.

Send

I Give Up

Did you find out what Tom's kids want?

Yes, he says his youngest is obsessed with sex dolls.

Haha! She is advanced for 9!!

I meant a Dexter doll, from Ever After High. Makes a change from Monster Pie.

Monster High. Or pie. Give up with this phone.

Send

Finally we have a decision! Your father likes Gay, which is disappointing but at least he's made up his mind.

You couldn't tell me in person? It's fine but this is a brutal way to hear.

On holiday. We are going to Gay on holiday. HAY! Hay-on-Wye!

Send

How is Dad feeling?

Much better, thank goodness. He had to go to Hotspur in the middle of the night.

??

Hot spice.

I am so fisted.

Frustrated.

DAD BACK FROM HOSPITAL. OK.

GOOD!

Send

What Cruise?

London is very tiring and after lunch we still have to do gent's anal cruise.

U should read that again.

Oopps! That was REGENTS C A N A L!

Sorry, almost dropped the phone. Dad is still laughing.

Send

Back   Contacts

It was lovely to see Caroline's grandchildren today. Her husband dressed up as Satan and the kids were very surprised.

I'm sure they were! LOL

Oh

He knows when they've been (VERY) naughty!

Send

Did you just try to call?

Not on purpose, sorry.

Must have been a booty call!!

Ha no! That is definitely NOT a booty call. Ass call, pocket dial, but not booty call, very different

Send

Love you.

Your mum.

Send